Get It Right

A Further Guide to Grammar

by Jackie Eyles
Illustrated by Lucy Maddison

Wayland

English Grammar

Start Right –
A First Guide to Grammar

Get It Right –
A Further Guide to Grammar

Editor: Katie Roden
Designer: Mark Whitchurch
Illustrator: Lucy Maddison
Consultant: Ian Enters, English Adviser, Curriculum and Staff
Development Service, Southfield Centre, Sheffield

First published in 1994 by
Wayland (Publishers) Ltd
61 Western Road, Hove
East Sussex BN3 1JD, England

British Library Cataloguing in Publication Data
    Eyles, Jackie
    Get It Right: A Further Guide to Grammar – (English
Grammar Series)
    I. Title II. Maddison, Lucy III. Series
    428.2

ISBN 0-7502-1265-9

Typeset by Mark Whitchurch
Printed and bound by Rotolito, Italy

National Curriculum Attainment Targets

Children at KS2 should be able to:

- write appropriately for a widening range of purposes and audiences;

- organize ideas into coherent and grammatically correct sentences;

- show a developing understanding of how writing can be improved;

- show increasing accuracy in the use of punctuation;

- use a widening, varied vocabulary;

- use the apostrophe to spell shortened forms of words;

- memorize the visual patterns of words, including those which are irregular.

All these skills are developed in this book.

Contents

Words in **bold** are explained in the glossary on page 30.

CHAPTER 1 Introduction

Writing is fun. This book will help you to write well.

Sid and Min will help make writing fun for you.

Writing is made up of words. The words are put into an order to make a **sentence**. Sentences begin with a **capital letter** and end with a **full stop**.

Look at my sentences about Sid. Try writing some sentences about your best friend. Draw a picture of your friend as well.

1. Sid has a very sharp point.
2. He loves ice-cream.
3. He writes quickly.
4. He can write very long stories.

This book has lots of games that will help you to be a good writer.

CHAPTER 2

Naming words: nouns

There are all kinds of words in a sentence. Words like cat, duck and sandwich are all naming words. These are called **nouns**.

Pick out the nouns from this list. You can find them all in the park.

cake	sun	very
duck	bike	see
tree	picnic	much
boat	milk	dog
green	write	ball

The answers are on page 32.

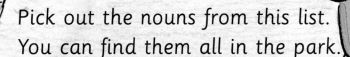

These sorts of nouns are called **common nouns** because people use them all the time. See if you can write some sentences about the park using common nouns.

6

Some nouns describe the names of people or places or special things. These nouns are called **proper nouns**. Words like Sid, Min and Tuesday are all proper nouns. They always begin with a capital letter.

WOOF!

Look at this sentence.

i am going to the park with **S**id and **m**in.

There are common nouns and proper nouns in this sentence. It should look like this:

I am going to the park with **S**id and **M**in.

Now see if you can spot the different nouns in these sentences. Which ones need capital letters?

You can find the answers on page 32.

On tuesday sid and min go to the park. The weather is very hot and min gets a suntan. sid says that he would like to live in a cold country like iceland.

Describing words: adjectives

Words like green, small, happy and strange are all **adjectives**. They are describing words.

Can you find the adjectives in the following list?

tree	cake	green
loud	milk	duck
pond	furry	eat
large	smooth	pond

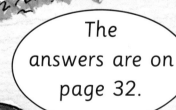

The answers are on page 32.

Look at the adjectives in these sentences. They describe our day at the park.

The park has a **large** pond.

Sid sits on a **big blue** blanket.

The duck has a **fluffy** tail.

The cake has **pink** icing.

The trees are **full** of **happy** birds.

Try writing some more sentences about our day in the park. See how many adjectives you can use.

Doing words: verbs

CHAPTER 4

Doing words are called verbs.

Look at the **verbs** in these sentences. They are the words written in red.

Min **runs** down the path.
The duck **swims** on the pond.
Sid **eats** a sandwich.
Min **drinks** some lemonade.

You can find all these doing words in the park. See if you can make up some sentences using them.

eat   play
falls   creeps
hides   swims
shouts   jumps

QUACK!

7, 8, 9...

10

1. a bell   bangs
2. ducks   patter
3. leaves   rings
4. a door   neighs
5. raindrops   quack
6. a horse   rustle

CHAPTER 5

Spelling patterns

There are some words that have the same beginnings or endings. These beginnings and endings give words special meanings. It's easy to spell words if we use spelling patterns!

Some groups of letters can be used in lots of different words. Look at these patterns:

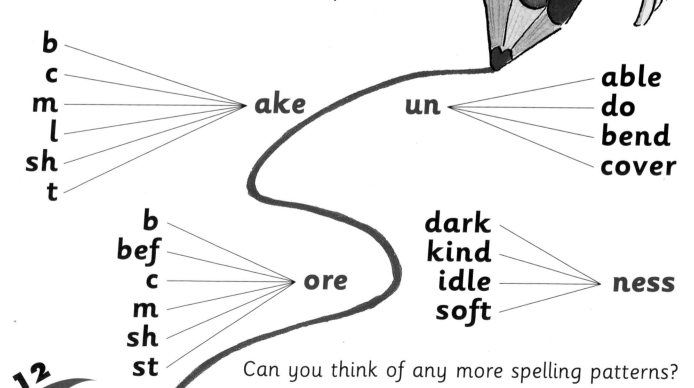

b
c
m
l
sh
t
→ **ake**

un ←
able
do
bend
cover

b
bef
c
m
sh
st
→ **ore**

dark
kind
idle
soft
→ **ness**

Can you think of any more spelling patterns?

'Un' words

When you add 'un' to a word, you give it an opposite meaning.

do	–	undo
able	–	unable
cover	–	uncover
equal	–	unequal

'Able' words

With 'able' you can turn a verb into an adjective.

agree	–	agreeable
enjoy	–	enjoyable
read	–	readable
change	–	changeable

'Ness' words

Adding 'ness' turns an adjective into a noun.

dark	–	darkness
kind	–	kindness
idle	–	idleness
soft	–	softness

Also look out for words beginning with **il**, **in** and **ir**. Look for words that end with **ship**, **hood**, **age**, **ing** and **ism**. See if you can work out what these beginnings and endings do to words.

13

Punctuation

> Now it's time to make our sentences more interesting. Punctuation will help us do this.

Commas

Commas separate parts of a sentence. They tell you when to pause for breath when you are reading:
Sid eats some candy-floss, then a toffee-apple, then a bar of chocolate.

Commas can also separate things in a list:
Min bought chips, fish, more chips and a drink.

See if you can put commas into these sentences:

Min went on the roundabout the swings the big wheel and the slide.

Sid tried to hit a coconut but his ball hit the ground instead.

> You can find the answers on page 32.

Apostrophes

You can make your sentences quicker to write and read by leaving out letters. You need an **apostrophe** to tell people you have done this.

do not	don't
can not	can't
they will	they'll
he is	he's

Look at these sentences. Can you change each word in blue for a word with an apostrophe?

Sid **can not** find Min.
They will soon go on the roundabout.
Sid and Min **do not** want to go home.
Sid is tired.

There are many more words which can use an apostrophe. Think about how you speak – you use lots of apostrophes!

See how many sentences you can write to describe our day at the fair. Try to use commas and apostrophes.

Question marks

You need **question marks** to show that you are asking a question. They go at the end of sentences.

Who is your best friend**?**
What is your favourite food**?**

Questions often begin with:
what, **who**, **why**,
where, **when**,
how, **will**.

Play a game with your friends. Write down some questions about our day at the fair. Show your friends the picture on pages 14 and 15, then hide it. Ask them your questions. See how many they can get right!

16

Exclamation marks

Exclamation marks go at the ends of sentences. They show anger or surprise. They can also tell you that someone is giving a command.

Speech marks

Speech marks are used when you write down something that someone has said.

They are found at the beginning and end of what has been said. Look at this example.

Sid says, **"**Do you want to go on the helter-skelter, Min?**"**

Min says, **"**Yes please!**"**

Look at these pictures of our day at the fair. Can you write a sentence for each picture, using speech marks?

Here is an example.

Min and Sid buy some ice-cream. Min says, "What flavour ice-cream do you like best?" Sid says, "Chocolate! Do you want one?"

Try and use all the things we've learnt so far in your sentences.

How to use writing

CHAPTER 7

Writing can be used in many different ways. Here are just a few of them.

Letters are a way of getting in touch with people. You can write letters to your friends to tell them all your news. You might need to write **formal** letters to important people.

Sid and Min are going on holiday to the seaside. Sid has to write a letter to a hotel to book some rooms. This is a formal letter.

When you write a letter, you must put your address at the top and your name at the bottom of the page. Make sure you put the name of the person you are writing to!

1 Scribble Row
Writetown
ABC 123

Dear Mr Smith,

Please can we book two rooms in your hotel. We will arrive on 16 April and will stay for three nights.

Yours sincerely,
Sid

At the seaside, Sid and Min write **postcards** to their friends. Postcards have pictures on the front and are not as formal as letters. You must put your friend's address on the back, though!

21

Lists

Lists are very useful. They help us to remember what we need to do or buy.

Here's my shopping list. Now I know what I need to buy in the shops.

Apples
Potatoes
Bread
Milk
Biscuits
Lemonade
Ice-cream
Shampoo

Make up some lists for these occasions.

What to take on holiday
Min's birthday party
Painting a house

Recipes are also useful. A recipe tells you how to make food. It has a list of all the **ingredients** and a description of how to make the food.

Try my special recipe for clown biscuits.

Clown biscuits

You will need
Digestive biscuits
Icing sugar
Sweets to decorate
A bowl
A knife

1. In the bowl, mix the icing sugar with enough water to make a smooth paste.
2. Spread the icing on the biscuits.
3. Use the sweets to make a clown face.

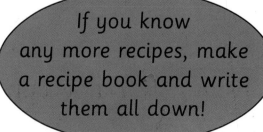

If you know any more recipes, make a recipe book and write them all down!

23

Stories

Writing stories is my favourite way of using writing!

To write a story you need lots of different words – nouns, adjectives and verbs. You also need to write in sentences.

Remember, a story must have a beginning, a middle and an end. It must also have a title, so everyone knows what it is about!

I have got a really good idea for a story. Why don't you write the story?

The Unhappy Monster
title

a monster	jungle	looks for a friend	finds another monster
character	**place**	**plot**	**ending**
beginning		**middle**	**end**

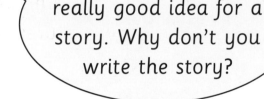

24

I bet you can write fantastic stories! Try writing some more, using these titles.

The cowardly pirate
A journey into space
The day time stood still
Sid's unlucky day

You could make a story book and draw pictures to brighten up your stories!

25

CHAPTER 8

Word games

You can use words to play games with your friends. **Riddles** can be really fun. See if you can solve these riddles.

I am big
I have a trunk
I am grey
What am I?

I am small
I have big ears
I have a long tail
I eat cheese
What am I?

I am red
I have black spots
I can fly
What am I?

I am black
I have eight legs
I spin a web
What am I?

You can find the answers on page 32.

Try writing some riddles for your friends. See if they can get them right.

I bet you can think of lots more riddles!

You can also make crosswords. You will need to think of clues to help your friends guess the right words. You must also use numbers to show them where each word goes.

I've made a treasure island crossword for Sid. He's nearly finished it.

One of the clues is missing. See if you can write it.

Try making up some more crosswords for your friends.

Clues
Across
2. The ship was tossed around in a tropical _ _ _ _ _
5. The _ _ _ _ _ was buried on the island.
6. Pirate maps were written in a _ _ _ _ _ code

Down
1. The secret _ _ _ _ _ _ was hard to crack
3. The pirate hid his face with a _ _ _ _ _
4.

Glossary

adjectives Describing words.

apostrophe A mark used to show where a letter or letters have been left out.

capital letter A letter used at the beginning of a sentence and for proper nouns.

commas Marks used to divide parts of a sentence. They allow the reader to pause.

common nouns Naming words. They are the names of common things, like cars and trees.

exclamation marks Marks used at the end of a sentence to show anger or surprise or give a warning or command.

formal Following a set of rules.

full stop A mark used for finishing a sentence.

ingredients All the different things that are mixed together to make food.

letters Written messages sent to people in the post.

lists words or sentences in an order.

nouns Naming words.

postcards Informal letters used to send messages to people. They are small cards with a picture on one side.

proper nouns Special naming words that always begin with a capital letter e.g. Sid, Min, Tuesday.

question marks Marks used at the end of a sentence when a question is being asked.

riddles Puzzling questions.

sentence A set of words that make sense, beginning with a capital letter and ending with a full stop.

speech marks These marks enclose something that has been spoken and then written down.

verbs Doing words that describe actions.

Books to read

Practise in the Basic Skills – English (series) by D. Newton and D. Smith (Collins, 1993)

English 7-12 (series) by D. Hughes and A. Josephs (Collins, 1993)

English Links (series) by Sheila Lane and Marion Kemp (Collins, 1992)

All About English by John and Elizabeth Seely (Oxford Primary Books, 1990)

Word Patterns (series) by Peter and Joan Moss (Collins, 1988)

The Usborne Book of English Grammar by R. Gee and C. Watson (Usborne, 1983)

Notes for parents and teachers

Children need to develop their skills of reading and writing. Once they have acquired the essential skills, these need to be refined and extended. Writing is a necessary skill needed for communication through all areas of the curriculum. This book extends the experience gained in Start Right. It is designed to help children extend and enjoy reading and, especially, writing. It allows children, with parents and teachers, to enjoy pages of activities that will develop writing skills. The child should have a book with pages of plain paper in which to carry out the activities, and access to a range of materials for making the games, cards etc.

The activities all focus on the requirements of the National Curriculum Programme of Study for English Key Stage 2: Writing.

To become fluent in reading and writing, children need to acquire skills and confidence. Parents and teachers can encourage the child by sharing the enjoyment of carrying out the activities in this book. Reading and writing should be fun!

Index

Answers

How many did you get right?

page 6 cake, duck, tree, boat, sun, bike, picnic, milk, dog, ball

page 7 On Tuesday **S**id and **M**in go to the park. The weather is very hot and **M**in gets a suntan. **S**id says that he would like to live in a cold country like Iceland.

page 8 Loud, large, furry, smooth, green

page 11 1. a bell **rings**
2. ducks **quack**
3. leaves **rustle**
4. a door **bangs**
5. raindrops **patter**
6. a horse **neighs**

page 14 Min went on the roundabout, the swings, the big wheel and the slide. Sid tried to hit a coconut, but his ball hit the ground instead.

page 15 Sid **can't** find Min.
They'll soon go on the roundabout.
Sid and Min **don't** want to go home.
Sid's tired.

page 26 The riddles are describing an elephant, a mouse, a ladybird and a spider.

32